Rule
of
Thumb

**A Small Business Guide to
Peak Performance Through People**

Rule of Thumb

A Small Business Guide to Peak Performance Through People

Todd A. Conkright, MA, CPT

Published by

WriteLife, LLC	Rule of Thumb
2323 S. 171 St.	3838 Davenport St
Suite 202	Lower Level
Omaha, NE 68130	Omaha, NE 68131
www.writelife.com	http://ruleofthumbbiz.com

Printed in the United States of America

ISBN 978 1 60808 077 9

First Edition

Contents

Why Rule of Thumb?

This book is part of the Rule of Thumb series produced in affiliation with the Rule of Thumb for Business whose mission is to "enrich business growth and development." The Rule of Thumb series offers basic information in plain language that will help you start, grow and sustain your business. The explanation for using the *"rule of thumb"* concept was introduced in the first book and is included again here.

Throughout history, a *"rule of thumb"* was used in measurements in a wide variety of businesses and vocations. The following list gives a few examples of how the thumb was used for measuring:

- In agriculture, the thumb was used to measure the depth at which to plant a seed.
- In restaurants and pubs, the thumb was used to measure the temperature of beer and ale.
- Tailors used the thumb to make sure enough space was allowed between the person's skin and his/her clothing. For example, the space between the cuff of the sleeve and the wrist had to be at least the width of the thumb.

- Carpenters used the width of the thumb rather than a ruler for measuring. For example, a notch in a board may need to be cut two thumb widths from the edge.

A *"rule of thumb"* is an idea or rule that may be applied in most situations, but not all. The *"rules of thumb"* in this book give you many reliable, convenient and simple rules that will help you remember many "dos" and "don'ts" that go with owning and running a business. Many of these concepts can also be used in a variety of business situations ranging from management, sales, customer service, human resources and leadership. The information is designed to be easy, simple and action-oriented. To learn more about the Rule of Thumb for Business organization visit our website at www.ruleofthumbbiz.com. – *Rule of Thumb for Business.*

Chapter 1
Introduction to Performance Management

As an organization grows and staff positions are added, the process of managing employee performance becomes more and more critical. The more proactive you are in managing performance the less of a drain it will be on your valuable time. In order for your organization to achieve its goals you need to ensure employees are meeting expectations on a regular basis. Performance gaps hit your business in many places:

- Customer service,
- Productivity,
- Quality, and
- Employee satisfaction

Allowing employees to perform below what your business needs creates a work environment of inconsistency, tension and frustration that eventually your customers will pick up on and choose to walk away from.

The good news is that there is a simple process you can follow that will ensure your employees

- Know what is expected of them
- Are held accountable for meeting expectations

- Understand the consequences of poor performances
- Actively participate in managing their own performance
- Use their strengths every day to help the company succeed

This book is your guide for implementing the performance management process so that you can get the most out of your employees. Here's what the process looks like visually:

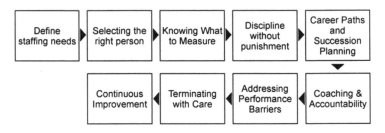

The important thing about performance management is that, when done well (consistently & intentionally), it can have a significant positive impact on your organization's success.

Consistency

Managers lose credibility when they are inconsistent in setting expectations and holding employees accountable for performance. This does not mean that every employee is treated exactly the same way, but it does mean using the same criteria and standards, and following through regularly.

When the manager's behavior is unpredictable, employees lose trust and their performance suffers. Create processes for managing performance and stick with them over time. When you see a need to change your focus or methods, communicate actively to explain what is changing and why.

Intentionally

To be intentional means to know the purpose behind what you are doing. Discover the best methods to manage employees and develop skill in applying them with your employees. This book provides a good foundation for understanding what works best in managing performance. You will want to make each of the approaches you read about in this book your own.

Your personality, as well as the personalities of your employees, will determine how you apply these best practices. Intentionally making an effort to learn and practice performance management processes shows your employees that you are willing to invest in them as individuals, making them much more likely to give their best efforts to help you and the organization succeed.

Every organization has a unique culture and circumstances, so use this book as a general guide. You might benefit from consulting with a performance management consultant to get specific advice.

Rule of Thumb:
Be consistent and intentional when managing employee performance

Chapter 2
Defining Staffing Needs

Performance management begins the moment you decide you need to hire someone to help you achieve your goals. This chapter introduces a useful process for knowing what positions to add and in what order. You will learn about planning your staffing needs ahead of time and how to begin putting together job descriptions.

Knowing how many people you need to hire and into which positions takes some preparation. Although some of your staffing may evolve organically as you start to expand your business, thinking through scenarios ahead of time will help you make better decisions in the moment. You may add a bookkeeper to help with administrative tasks so that you can focus on sales, or you may hire a second salesperson as you move into new markets, or if you are in a manufacturing operation, equipment will often dictate how many people you need, depending on the output you need to produce and what it takes to keep up with the increased production. Whatever the scenario, consider what additional positions will help you achieve your goals.

The best approach to intentional staffing is to create a matrix that shows incremental additions to your company as you grow. The example below shows the threshold levels for three different jobs. Remember, your matrix may change as new opportunities, needs, or challenges surface.

Table 1-1 Staffing Needs Matrix

Position	Up to $1m revenue	$1 -5m	$5-10m
Outside Sales	1	2	3
Office Support	1	1.5	2
Management	1	1	2

Sales revenue may never increase past a certain level if additional salespeople are not hired, but as they bring in more business, it will take more office support to process orders, manage customer support, and keep things running behind the scenes. At some point, additional managers are needed to supervise the growing staff.

Job Descriptions

What most small business owners and managers overlook is the need to design job descriptions as the company grows in order to avoid ambiguity and territorial disputes. When people are unclear about their responsibilities and boundaries, they may become defensive on one hand or reluctant on the other. Take the time now to put in writing the primary functions of each position. You should review job descriptions annually, especially if you are experiencing rapid growth.

At some point you will find the need to either create new jobs as the workload becomes too much for one person to manage, or hire additional people into the same role. If you are thinking about adding a position but do not know how to divide up the tasks, check with companies of similar size in your industry to see how they structure their staff. Assume you will need to customize your roles to fit your company, but if you can avoid re-creating the wheel by leveraging what someone else has done, you can stay focused on more important business activities.

We will talk more about individual strengths in the next chapter, but it is important to identify the strengths and skills needed to successfully accomplish the purpose for each position as you create job descriptions and expand your staff. It may seem obvious, but it does not make sense to hire someone that does not have the capacity, interest or skill to do the job. Yet many managers make this mistake by not considering what type of individual is needed for a particular job. It is also important to be careful not to assume that because someone was successful in a similar job they will fit well with another organization.

Consider company culture, and structure, and the direction the organization is heading to determine if a potential employee is a good choice. It will save a lot of disappointment and frustration for you and them by being cautious now.

Friends and Family

Be careful about hiring friends and family. Take the same care to place them in the best position for their qualifications and interests as you would someone you do not know. Avoid the temptation to populate your organization with relatives and friends – it is hard to manage or fire them if they do not work out.

As you can tell, making staffing decisions is as much about "how many" as it is about "who." If you have not grown large enough to hire a full-time human resources professional, consider hiring an HR consultant to get advice on staffing and selection. If you have an office manager or other administrative person in charge of hiring and staffing, encourage them to join the local chapter of the Society for Human Resource Management (SHRM) and educate themselves on HR laws, recruiting and staffing best practices, and other human resources functions.

Checklist for Defining Staffing Needs
- Create 3-5 year growth projection
- Identify positions to support growth goals
- Begin job description process by knowing what is required for added positions

- Hold family and friends to same standards & qualifications

Rule of Thumb:
Take the time now to put in writing the primary functions of each position.

Chapter 3
Right Person, Right Job

In the previous chapter you learned that having the right person in the right job is critical to the success of your business. To reduce the frustration and disruption to your business of hiring a poorly-suited employee, identify competencies, skills & abilities necessary for each role and how to select the right individual. Also recognize the personal qualities and values that define your organization's culture and know how to determine if someone is a good fit.

The important thing about finding the right person for the right job is taking the time to do the work required. It means reflecting on what your company stands for and the types of people that will help you carry those values forward.

Knowledge, Skills & Abilities (KSAs)

The best place to start when it comes to selecting employees is with the required knowledge, skills & abilities (KSAs). As a growing company, you may choose to hire someone with minimal KSAs and train them along the way. The advantage of this approach is that you won't have to pay at the top of the wage or salary level. That person is groomed and trained as your company expands and they become an expert in your processes & industry.

There is a temptation to hire someone at an entry-level wage and experience level, but the disadvantage of hiring someone with minimal knowledge, skills & abilities is that you get just that – minimal knowledge, skills and abilities! They may have great potential, but you may not have the time or resources to train them properly and could miss out on the talents of a more experienced person.

What knowledge does someone need in order to be a success today? Do they need to understand a particular industry? Know the latest technology or equipment? Have experience with a specialized process? Do they need knowledge about marketing, sales, accounting, or customer service? If they cannot acquire the knowledge within a few weeks on the job, can you afford to have them below full capacity for an extended period of time?

Skills and abilities are the application of knowledge. Someone may have been in customer service for years at another small business, but did they do it well? How do you know if they can perform at the level you need them to? You will want to ask some very specific questions as you interview candidates. It is also extremely important to check references.

Competencies

Korn/Ferry, a leader in the field of workplace competencies, defines competencies as *the skills, behaviors, and attitudes that lead to high performance.* (Lombardo, 2009)

Defining competencies for a specific job takes some skill, but there are resources available to help you identify what competencies will lead to the best performance from the individuals in your organization. Trying to find a well-rounded person with a cross-section of competencies may not be best for your success. Hiring an accountant who can also sell may sound like a great "two for one" deal, but you might end up with a mediocre accountant or a frustrated salesperson.

Follow these steps to identify the job competencies for each position in your organization:

1. Make several copies of the competency list in Appendix A. On one of the copies circle the top 10 competencies you believe are necessary to be successful in that job.

2. Narrow the list down to 5-6 of the most critical competencies. Get the opinion of others. If there is already someone doing the job, ask them for their input. What do they think is required?

3. If you have a job description already, review it to see if what you circled matches with what the job description reflects. If they

do not match, what is different? Make any adjustments based on your review.

4. Use your finalized list as a guide as you think through anyone already in the position as well as who you might hire for that job in the future. (We'll talk about what to do if the person in the job is not a good fit based on what you have identified).

Identifying Strengths

There are several books available that talk about strengths, including Strengths 2.0 from Gallup and Standout from Marcus Buckingham. Strengths and competencies are closely related. What is important about strengths is that we want to understand what a person does well on a consistent basis and how that impacts what job responsibilities are best for them.

Once you identify the strengths necessary for a position and match a job applicant who has those strengths, both the organization and the candidate win! They will be motivated and eager to make your organization successful because they are using their strengths on a regular basis.

Values & Culture Fit

An often-overlooked, but extremely important consideration as you try to put the right person in the right job, is how that person fits with your organization's culture, including values and mission.

The fancy term for this is "values congruence," which simply refers to a match between organization values and individual values. Assuming your organization has identified their values – what is important to you, how you want to operate your business, the ethical and moral principles you operate within, and the reputation you want to have with employees, customers and the community – then you will find it easier to determine if someone you want to hire is a good fit.

You will also want to look at your organization's culture. If you are a very structured, hierarchical company, you may not want to hire someone who likes to do things their own way and works "outside the box." If you have a creative, unstructured workplace where rules are less important, hiring someone who likes structure and order may set them up for frustration and failure. Of course, if you are at one extreme and want to move the other direction (from overly structured to more free-flowing), then make sure if you are hiring specifically to get new blood in the system that the person knows you want to use them as a model and make it an intentional process. Otherwise, you will end up with a confused, frustrated and unproductive team.

Rule of Thumb:
Do the work of reflecting on what your company stands for and the types of people that will help carry those values forward.

Right Fit Checklist

Use this checklist as you interview candidates for jobs. To avoid bias, have a business partner or trusted friend go through the list with you.

- Personality fits with our organization
- Values align with our values
- Their strengths are needed for this position
- They have required
  - ☐ Knowledge
  - ☐ Skills
  - ☐ Abilities
- I have asked the right questions to determine competencies and fit
- I have checked professional references and/or seen samples of work

Chapter 4
Knowing What to Measure

Holding your staff accountable for reaching performance goals is essential to your success. Knowing what to measure is as simple as knowing why the position exists in the first place. If you have gone through the previous steps of defining your staffing needs and putting the right person in the right job, the next step should be easy. What makes it complicated is a lack of clarity in what needs to be accomplished and in what timeframe. If you hire a salesperson and do not give them a sales goal or territory, they will not be nearly as successful as they could be. We need goals to keep us focused, mark progress, and motivate us to push to higher levels.

The best way to create success measurements for each position is to start with the job description. What do you need this position for? If you own a retail shop and you hire a customer service associate, you need them to

- Share product knowledge with customers
- Promote items and suggest add-ons
- Ring up the sale and process credit card transactions

- Give the customer a great experience so they'll come back again
- Keep the shop neat and clean
- Answer the phone

You can probably think of more, but let's take a look at these six tasks and how we can measure performance.

Table 4-1 Staffing Needs Matrix

Task	Measurements
Share product knowledge	Mystery shopper scores, customer feedback,
Promote items and suggest add-ons	Track overall sales productivity (sales per hour), sales on specific items (spiffs)
Ring up sales	Accuracy & efficiency, data from POS terminal, reports
Give the customer a great experience	Mystery shopper scores, customer feedback,
Keep the shop neat & clean	Task checklists & audits
Answer the phone	Number of rings to answer

Measurement is effective only when it is specific, clearly communicated, and most importantly, tied to what is important to your business. You can measure just about anything, but that doesn't mean you should. Focus on a few metrics that align with your organizational goals. Think about how each position contributes to the bottom line. What is it that has the potential to enhance your productivity, make you the customer service leader, open up the markets you're interested in, and make your organization lean and laser focused?

To get the most out of your employees they need to know what is important. Measure and recognize what you want to see more of. No one can process a pile of feedback and figure out what is important to you if you give feedback on everything. A scorecard or productivity report that has more than 5-6 key metrics will overwhelm and confuse employees. What are the key performance indicators (KPIs) that they should care about?

Key Performance Indicators (KPIs) are what tell you whether you are on the right track as a company. Start by identifying your organization-level KPIs, then do the same thing for every position. The individual KPIs should directly support the organization's KPIs. Some examples of organization-level KPIs are provided in the table on the next page.

Table 4-2 Staffing Needs Matrix

Type of Organization	KPI Example
Fitness Club	Conversions from introductory package to regular membership
Clothing Store	Percentage of sales from repeat customers
Manufacturing Company	Machine uptime (at full capacity)
Inbound Call Center	Average speed of answer, handle time
Drive-through Restaurant	Seconds from order to delivery
Web Designer	Percentage increase in web traffic (hits)

There are KPI banks available online that can help you develop the measurements that are right for you. A couple of good online resources are The Advanced Performance Institute (www.ap-institute.com) and The KPI Library (http://kpilibrary.com/). Both sites require you to create a free account and were active as of September, 2012.

As you develop organizational and individual measurements, keep these things in mind:

1. **Know why you are measuring what you are measuring.** Is your goal to develop or control employees? Metrics are a snapshot of performance, but may not tell the whole story.

2. **Limit what you measure to what is most critical.** There may be 10+ activities tied to a position, but try to narrow down what you

measure to 5-6. What outcomes are the tasks supporting? Let that be the KPI.

3. **Create a scorecard report that shows performance over time.** Everyone can have a really stellar or dismally poor week, month, quarter. Have a long-term view of performance and use the scorecard to help you learn about what may be getting in the way of performance and guide you to the solution.

Learning Curve

It is important to give a new employee (including a transfer employee from one role in your organization to another) a reasonable learning curve, at the end of which they should be performing at full capacity. You should not assume that most new employees can walk in the door and be able to perform as well as a tenured employee. Depending on the complexity of the job, length of formal training, and historical experience on how long others have taken to get up to speed, you can expect 3 weeks to 6 months for a learning curve.

Whenever possible, adjust initial performance measurements based on the individual's progress toward full performance capacity. If you have a particularly sharp, energetic and motivated new-hire, they may breeze through the learning curve much faster than the average new employee. And keep in mind that just because someone is a little slower than average in getting up to speed does not mean that they will not be an excellent employee once they gain confidence and experience. Everyone learns differently, and your expectations should be adjusted based on the individual.

Rule of Thumb:
Measurement is effective only when it is specific, clearly communicated, and most importantly, tied to what is important to your business.

Checklist for Creating Performance Measures
- Identify tasks that should be measured for each position.
- Identify how you will measure each task.
- Create a scorecard or productivity report with 6 or fewer metrics.
- Know what the average learning curve is for each job.

Chapter 5
Recognizing and Rewarding Contributions

Recognition is a crucial piece of the employee motivation puzzle. But it is more than giving movie tickets for meeting a sales goal. To be effective, recognition and rewards need to be meaningful to the recipient, motivate them to continue achieving goals, and support organizational objectives.

Achievements, even routine ones that are not "above and beyond," deserve to be called out for recognition. It keeps people engaged and lets them know that you are aware when they are productive and actively contributing to the organization. Of course, you should reserve special awards and recognition for times when individuals and groups go above expectations. Often a hand-written note from the top boss or owner, or a "drive-by" thank you is enough. For major sales, significant breakthroughs, or particularly grueling projects, a cash award or large non-monetary prize is warranted.

If you keep a scorecard, as suggested earlier, you can tie achievement of scorecard standards to rewards and recognition. For example, you might contribute a dollar amount to a fund for every quarter (or month, or week) in which goals are met.

Contests and stretch goals are also a good way to motivate employees to perform at higher levels. Make the goals realistic, but require more than normal effort to achieve them. If you make the goals too hard to achieve you may discourage employees from even trying because they don't think it is possible to hit the target. Goals should not be too easy either, or you will be handing out special recognition for routine work.

It is also important to recognize anniversaries (with the company and personal), birthdays, and other special occasions. Recognition of these milestones does not have to be expensive. Even a hand-written card sent to the home, or simply stopping by the person's desk to congratulate or thank them will go a long way in building a culture of recognition, which leads to satisfaction and engagement from your employees.

Typically any award with a cash value of over one hundred dollars (whether cash or non-cash) is taxable and has to be reflected as income on the person's W2. Many companies cover the taxes so a gift will not be worth less than intended. For instance, if you are giving a $150 spiff, you might actually give $185, or whatever amount will ensure that the cash amount comes out to $150. Employees will grumble if their $150 is only worth $120 after taxes! Check current tax laws for your location(s) to make sure you are in compliance.

You may have some employees who are self-motivated and seem to not desire feedback. They are embarrassed by group recognition and may even appear hostile if they are singled out for awards or appreciation. In most cases, it doesn't mean that they don't want their performance acknowledged, only that they prefer a low-key, private approach. They still want to know they are meeting your expectations.

Many managers are of the mindset that it is not important to provide recognition when employees are simply doing what they were hired to do. Their paycheck and continued employment are reward enough for meeting the expectations of the job, right? While this sounds logical, the fact is, employees need feedback on their performance, whether they are meeting, exceeding or missing expectations.

Some tips to make sure your recognition program is motivating:

1. Make rewards meaningful to the recipient(s)
2. Consider how to personalize recognition
3. Tie recognition to organizational objectives & values
4. Use contests from time-to-time to spark excitement
5. Make sure the reward or recognition matches the level of effort or impact

Group Incentives

Many companies offer team rewards, incentives tied to group performance. There are pros and cons of this approach. On the pro side, group incentives can promote camaraderie and teamwork, improve innovation, and energize the work group. When designed well, teams are excited to work together, contributing their strengths and expertise for the benefit of the organization.

The reality is, if an individual has done well, there are usually others who have enabled that success. Group incentives can help recognize everyone who has worked on a project to make it successful.

Managed poorly, group incentives can have the opposite impact. They can tear a team apart when a perception exists that someone isn't pulling his or her weight. Instead of avoiding group incentives as a way to avoid this risk, the best companies build a culture that encourages everyone to contribute their best effort. Strong leadership is required. This does not mean coercive or hard-line tactics are used, but leadership that makes people want to do their best, to be fully engaged.

There are two types of group incentives: gain-sharing and goal-sharing. Gain-sharing plans are tied directly to the bottom line and can be in the form of cost savings or revenue generation. You might ask a manufacturing group to reduce operating expenses by ten percent and fund an incentive with some of the savings. In this way they are self-funded and the more the group is able to save or generate, the larger the reward.

In goal-sharing, groups are asked to make

improvements in customer satisfaction, program effectiveness. Funding for goal-sharing plans are not typically self-funding and come out of the operating budget.

In both gain-sharing and goal-sharing plans, predetermined performance measurements, timelines, and guidelines are critical to success of the program.

Checklist for Recognition and Reward Program

- Make a commitment to recognize performance routinely
- Create contests and stretch goals that are realistic.
- Make incentives meaningful and worthy of extra effort.
- Learn the payroll laws related to incentives and rewards.

> **Rule of Thumb:**
> To be effective, recognition and rewards need to be meaningful to the recipient, motivate them to continue achieving goals, and support organization objectives.

Chapter 6
Coaching & Accountability for Maximum Performance

Coaching and accountability go hand-in-hand. Once you have communicated performance expectations and goals, you hold employees accountable for meeting those expectations. Coaching provides feedback on what they have done well and what they need to improve. Accountability comes first, and coaching is used as a tool to hold people accountable.

Accountability

Accountability is a finance term – giving an account means showing what is in the debit column and what is in the credit column. From a performance management view, then, accountability is about measuring the profit or loss of the employee's performance effort. That is not to say we are putting the person in the profit or loss column, but simply evaluating contributions through the tasks and responsibilities of the individuals.

Accountability has a lot to do with integrity, specifically trustworthiness and dependability. Do we do what we say we will do? Accountability is taking responsibility for our actions and fulfilling the expectations we have either directly or indirectly promised to complete. Look at these examples of direct and indirect promises.

Direct Accountability

Your sales manager, John, has promised to turn in his expense report by Friday at 4 p.m. Now he is accountable for completing the report on or before Friday afternoon. He can hold himself accountable by making sure he blocks out enough time to meet the deadline. You can also hold him accountable by checking with him before the deadline to make sure he's still planning to meet his commitment to you. Of course, you don't want to nag or micromanage John, since that can cause tension and needless pressure.

If John meets the deadline you will thank him for his promptness, which will set the tone for him wanting to meet the deadline in the future. If he is late with the report, you need to restate your expectations and the consequences of his noncompliance: others may be waiting on him to do their part in the process, there could be a delay in reimbursing him, the message that his missing the deadline sends about how he views his job, etc..

Indirect Accountability

Karen is your office receptionist. Her duties and tasks vary from day-to-day and because she has a wide range of responsibilities it's hard to make a list of everything. Her job description gives a big picture view of her position and highlights a lot of her priorities, but it's not a complete list. When Karen receives assignments from you, or handles things in the course of her day that aren't specifically detailed in her job description, she is holding herself accountable to the spirit of her position.

As her boss, holding her accountable will take some open communication. You may assume something falls into her responsibilities, but she may believe that it's outside the scope of her job. Since it's not a specific task on her list of job duties, you want to talk with her about why you see it as her responsibility and listen to her explanation of why she thinks it is not.

With indirect accountability, you can see that the "ownership" of following through on things rests with the person who assumes responsibility. They hold themselves accountable, but you can also hold them accountable to the extent that you have communicated general principles and expectations.

Accountability in the workplace helps create order, ensures standards are met, and keeps people doing what needs to be done in order for your business to succeed. Lack of accountability often leads to chaos, territorialism, and infighting. That's not good for your business, because it means a lot of energy is being used to point fingers, avoid responsibility, and do just enough to get by.

A culture of accountability will lead to greater productivity, job satisfaction and

Coaching

Most managers approach coaching from the perspective of telling the employee what they're doing wrong and giving them guidance or ultimatums to fix their performance deficiencies. This creates an adversarial relationship between manager and employee, and both sides end up dreading the "coaching session." What I recommend is a positive coaching model that brings out the best in the employee as you identify their strengths, successes and potential.

This requires the manager to change the lens through which they see their employees. If you are only looking for what someone is doing wrong, poorly, or needs improvement on, you will begin to see that person in terms of their weaknesses and failings. But if you start looking for what they do well, what they have succeeded at, and the potential they have to perform above and beyond what is expected of them, then you will begin to see them as a valuable asset to your company.

Getting Performance Data

A common challenge many companies face is the lack of direct observation by bosses of their subordinates. Whether an eating establishment with varying shifts, virtual "work at home" setups, or salespeople and contractors who rarely come into the office, managers need to give coaching and feedback to employees they don't spend much direct face-to-face time with. In order to effectively coach in these circumstances, the manager has to collect performance information from other sources.

> **Rule of Thumb:**
> Start looking for what employees do well, what they have succeeded at, and the potential they have to perform above and beyond what is expected of them, then you will begin to see them as a valuable asset to your company.

Customers and colleagues are a good source of information, but be careful that you weigh this type of feedback with your own observations and impressions. If you're hearing extremes of excellent or poor performance, make sure you ask multiple sources to verify the reliability of the information. You don't want to base coaching on feedback from a single person who likely has his own biases.

Get facts as well as stories. If you have performance measurements, those should be a starting point for your coaching. How is the individual performing against the goals? Against others? Are there special projects or circumstances that have impacted their regular performance? Were their goals adjusted? The bottom line is this: be fair and reasonable as you evaluate the facts and stories about someone's performance.

Types of Coaching

Once you have gathered the performance data you can prepare for coaching. There are two types of coaching: structured and unstructured. In structured coaching you will actually sit down with your employees to discuss their performance and develop an action plan and goals. In unstructured coaching you're taking advantage of "coaching moments" that come about throughout the course of your interactions with employees. Instead of waiting for a scheduled coaching meeting, you will do "drive by" coaching to give immediate feedback.

Unstructured Coaching

Unstructured, drive-by coaching is intended to be positive and specific. For example, if you just got an email from a client praising your employee for exemplary service, there's no sense in waiting for a meeting to talk to that employee about how proud you are of the way they have represented the company. You may want to do more to recognize their performance through a bonus, hand-written thank-you note, or some other formal expression of your gratitude, but don't pass up an opportunity to recognize the employee right away, preferably in-person.

Developmental drive-by coaching requires a bit

more practice to make sure it comes across as helpful and positive. If you've just hung up the phone after talking with an irate customer because their delivery was late, you want to slow down before running over to the cubicle of the person who was charged with getting the delivery on time. Take a deep breath and try to get a big picture. Ask yourself a few questions, such as:

- Has this happened before with this employee?
- Could there be a misunderstanding about the delivery date and time?
- Are there other circumstances outside the employee's control that might have caused a delay?
- How can I use this situation to improve the employee and our customer satisfaction in the future?

Gather the facts and think through the questions above before you meet with the employee. Although the customer is upset and claiming your company failed, there may be a good or reasonable explanation. Perhaps your employee tried to contact the customer to let them know that there was a delay from the shipping company, or they talked with his assistant two days ago but he forgot to pass along the information to the boss. Any number of scenarios could have impacted the customer's experience, so wait until both sides are explained before assuming your employee is completely at fault.

When you meet with your employee you should start by calmly explaining the conversation you had with the customer. A good opening statement is "I just had a call from Joe Customer. He was pretty upset because his order wasn't delivered on time, which puts him behind on his work. Can you help me understand what went wrong so that we can salvage Joe's experience?" You are not blaming the employee, only asking for an explanation so you can find out what went wrong and how to fix it.

Structured Coaching

There are three parts to structured coaching: preparation, the coaching discussion, and follow-up. We tend to focus on the second part, the coaching discussion, and give little attention to preparation and even less to follow-up. All three of these steps is important. It may seem like a big time commitment, but with a little time management you will see the results are well worth the effort.

While unstructured coaching can happen at any time, structured coaching is pre-planned, at least two-three times/month (weekly is strongly suggested). Whenever possible, coaching sessions should be recurring meetings on your calendar that you make every effort to not reschedule or cancel. When you cancel or always move these meetings it sends a message to your employees that you do not value them or respect their time. Find a convenient time that works for both you and your employees and stick with it. Before or after regular business hours if you're a retailer are best, or choose a slow traffic day. Include the employee in deciding when to meet.

Coaching sessions do not have to be very long. If you are meeting weekly, a 15-minute session three times a month and a 30-minute session once a month works well. That way you can follow up on progress regularly. Once you have figured out a good schedule that works for you and your employee(s) you'll want to prepare for the coaching session.

We touched on the need for preparation in the Unstructured Coaching section above. With Structured Coaching, preparation is essentially the same. You will want to gather facts and stories related to the employee's performance, taking information from different sources and considering circumstances and outside factors that could have impacted performance. Review the employee's performance over a 3-6 month window, not just the past 2-4 weeks. The wider angle view you get of their performance over time the more realistic it is.

> ### *Rule of Thumb:*
> Keep a performance folder for each employee. As you get emails, reports, or any type of information about the performance, you can simply put it in the folder, then review and organize it prior to the coaching meeting.

Keeping a performance folder, whether paper or electronic, for each employee is a good idea. As you get emails, reports, or any type of information about the performance, you can simply put it in the folder, then review and organize it prior to the coaching meeting. Do a little research on those things that are out of the norm and come up with 2-3 questions to ask the employee about the situation.

Use a simple form, like the one at the end of the chapter, to help you prepare for the coaching session. Again, this can be paper or electronic. It is recommended that you create your own template that makes sense for the types of things you want to measure and coach on. You will want to include any carry-over items from previous coaching sessions, the current focus, and a historical record of 3-6 month performance results.

A tendency of some managers is to give employees a laundry list of things to work on. This can be very de-motivating and counter-productive. At most, three performance improvement topics can be managed at one time. Consider this example:

Jenny has 4-5 things she could improve, such as follow-up with clients, tracking orders in a timely manner, and communication with the manufacturing department. You have shared your expectations but she continues to struggle with these things. She'll do better on tracking orders one month, and worse on communication at the same time. What do you do to get her to meet the expectations in each area?

Try focusing on the most important issue and put the other ones on the back burner. If you believe that customer follow-up should be the top priority, work with Jenny on a solution and action plan, and each week when you meet with her go over her progress, fine-tune the plan, and congratulate her on any success. We'll discuss this topic further in the chapter titled *Discipline Without Punishment*. The important thing to remember is that the more you involve the employee in the solution, the more likely they will be to follow through.

The Coaching Discussion

When it comes to coaching, remember that it's not all about you! Coaching is about the other person – what you can do to guide, inform and encourage their progress. The recommended ratio for coach to employee is 30:70. That's right, you should only be speaking thirty percent of the time. You want to spend that thirty percent drawing out thoughts, ideas and solutions from the person you're coaching. That means asking lots of good questions. Here's an example:

Troy has been a software developer for your company for just over a year. He's creative, industrious and quick to respond to the needs of the organization. You gave him a project three weeks ago that you haven't seen much movement on. He seems stuck and you're not sure what is holding him back. You have noticed a strain with his co-workers and happened to walk by Troy's desk when he was uncharacteristically abrupt with a colleague from another department.

It's fifteen minutes before your weekly coaching session and you are not quite sure how to handle it. Keeping in mind that you're supposed to let Troy do most of the talking, you quickly write out some questions that might help get to the bottom of the issue.

Questions to Kick of Your Coaching Session with Troy:

- Tell me about your week. What's going well and what challenges are you facing?
- What progress have you made on the project I assigned to you recently? Is there anything preventing you from moving forward? What roadblocks might be in your way?
- How are you getting along with your peers? I thought I noticed some tension between you and Rebecca a few minutes ago.

These questions will open up a useful dialogue where you can help Troy identify what is keeping him from moving forward on the project and causing tension with his colleagues. Ask follow-up questions and help Troy identify the issues for himself. One of the challenges with being a manager is that there is a tendency to want to jump in with the cause and the solution. When you let the employee discover these for him- or herself, they develop the skill to identify issues themselves and become less dependent on you.

Following are additional questions that help get a coaching session started on the right foot, and put the focus on the employee rather than your checklist.

1. How are you doing right now?
2. Is there anything you would like to share with me before we start?
3. What are you most proud of this week?
4. What is the most valuable thing you have learned in the past 10 days?
5. Tell me how you went about getting that deal finalized with _____.
6. When have you felt you were most engaged and energized about your work this week?

Figure 6-1: Sample Coaching Form

Date: September 13, 2012

Employee: Kevin T.

Coaching Prep Checklist:
- Review performance scorecard
- Identify successes/positive feedback since last meeting
- Update progress on carry-over items
- List any opportunity areas to discuss with employee

Scorecard:

Sales Goal/ Actual	Prospects Goal/Actual	CRM Updates Goal/Actual	Client Follow up Goal/ Actual
150/153	12/15	15/8	10/7

Carry-Over from Last Coaching Session:

We discussed Kevin's challenges with the new CRM software program and Kevin agreed to watch the tutorial video to see if it might help him. He also agreed to ask Sylvia for help if he got stuck. He promised to have the tutorial completed by 9/8 and be up-to-speed on the software by the time we meet again on the 13th.

New Items:
- Congratulate Kevin on surpassing his sales goal – ask him what led to his success.

- Ask Kevin about prospects that he met with and how I might help him move them toward making a decision for our product.

- Find out how he is feeling about the new CRM software. Point out that he is still behind on his updates and ask him for a commitment date to be caught up.

- Ask him to explain why he is behind on client follow-ups but ahead on prospects. Explain the importance of following up with current clients and the balance with new prospects.

Goals for next coaching session: (determined together with employee)

Chapter 7
Formal Performance Appraisals

Everyone seems to hate performance appraisals. Ask most managers about the process and you will hear about how time consuming, insignificant and bothersome it is. And employees will tell you pretty much the same thing. They do not see much of a connection between what they do on a day-to-day basis and the feedback they hear on an annual basis from their managers. So how do managers make formal performance meaningful to employees? How can the appraisal process become something that both managers and employees find useful?

While some businesses are considering ditching performance reviews altogether, I suggest you consider how to do them well instead. First, we have to stop thinking about performance appraisals as a necessary evil. Companies tend to view them as documentation that can either justify decisions or protect the company if a person files a grievance. When bosses look at performance appraisals this way it removes any power they might have to manage performance in any productive way.

In many cases performance ratings do not truly

reflect the performance of the individual. Instead, they put everyone in the middle. If you truly have a staff of mediocre performers, you have some big problems in how you are selecting talent for your organization! In reality, managers are afraid to rate someone too low or too high and opt for the middle ground. Some companies will even instruct managers to not use the top rating because "no one is perfect." So we send the message that the expectation is a "5" but no one can actually achieve it!

Another thing that happens during the annual performance review is that employees get blindsided. This happens when a manager has not communicated with the employee that their performance is below standards – they do not find out until they sit down for their appraisal meeting and it's too late to do anything. There should be no surprises on the performance review. Instead, it should reflect a summary of all of the coaching and feedback you have provided in the previous 12 months.

In addition to the tendency to rate everyone as "average" on their performance appraisals, beware of biases that are not only unfair, but potentially illegal. The following list is based on a full list of biases that can be found at www.rationalwiki.org (active link as of September, 2012).

- **Bandwagon effect** — the tendency to do (or believe) things because many other people do (or believe) the same.

- **Confirmation bias** — the tendency to look for "proof" that what we believe is true.
- **Extreme aversion** — most people will go to great lengths to avoid extremes. People are more likely to choose an option if it is the intermediate choice.
- **Focusing effect** — prediction bias occurring when people place too much importance on one aspect of an event; causes error in accurately predicting the utility of a future outcome.
- **Framing** - drawing different conclusions from the same information, depending on how that information is presented.
- **Selective perception** — the tendency for expectations to affect perception.
- **Ambiguity effect** — the avoidance of options for which missing information makes the probability seem "unknown".
- **Anchoring** — the tendency to rely too heavily, or "anchor," on a past reference or on one trait or piece of information when making decisions.
- **Attentional bias** — neglect of relevant data when making judgments of a correlation or association.
- **Hindsight bias** — sometimes called the "I-knew-it-all-along" effect: the inclination to see past events as being predictable, based on

knowledge of later events.

- **Primacy effect** — the tendency to weigh initial events more than subsequent events.
- **Recency effect** — the tendency to weigh recent events more than earlier events (see also 'peak-end rule').
- **Rosy retrospection** — the tendency to rate past events more positively than they had actually rated them when the event occurred.
- **Halo effect** — the tendency for a person's positive or negative traits to "spill over" from one area of their personality to another in others' perceptions of them (*see also physical attractiveness stereotype*).
- **Illusion of transparency** — people overestimate others' ability to know them, and they also overestimate their ability to know others.

Five Steps to Meaningful Performance Appraisals

Doing performance appraisals the right way, meaning that they are a useful part of your performance management process, involves just a few simple principles.

1. **Communicate regularly about performance.** Through structured and unstructured coaching, keep lines of communication open. That way there won't be any surprises and employees will always know how they

are performing. Regularly recognize their strengths and successes and don't sugar-coat opportunities.

2. **Keep records of performance.** Keep a file for each employee, electronic and/or paper, to track performance issues. Get in the habit of writing down successes as well as opportunities. Tracking performance throughout the year ensures you're looking at the full twelve-month period and not the most recent record. Compare employees to the standards you've set, not to one another.

3. **Take the performance appraisal process seriously.** Schedule time to write appraisals and don't wait until the last minute. Start early and add to the document as things occur to you.

4. **Schedule enough time for the appraisal meeting.** Try meeting in a conference room or some other place other than your office to avoid distractions and set the right tone for the meeting.

5. **Actually review the appraisal with your employee.** Don't just hand the employee the form, or email it to them, print a copy for each of you, go through each section. Take the opportunity to praise them (again) for their successes and remind them of the items that you will continue to coach them on.

Pay Increases and Bonuses

Companies often use the annual performance review process to award pay increases and bonuses, which makes sense. Some companies are less transparent than others about what it takes to earn the highest level of increase. It makes managers nervous to put something in writing, in case funding is reduced and you won't be able to stick with the plan as communicated. To employees this is seen as a carrot – just out of reach so they'll keep chasing it! One solution is to include a statement that says, in effect, "this plan is not a guarantee, but a set of guidelines to communicate how performance is linked to pay…"

Rule of Thumb:
There should be no surprises on the performance review. Instead, it should reflect a summary of all the coaching and feedback you have provided in the previous 12 months.

Chapter 8
Career Paths & Succession Plans

Regular assessment of employees and consideration for advancing their career through a well-defined process provides momentum. Creating "bench strength" ensures you're always prepared if someone leaves the company or is moved to another position. (Bench Strength refers to the available talent waiting "on the bench" when someone moves into a new position or leaves the company) On the other hand, if you wait until someone leaves to begin thinking about who might step in to fill their role, you may find that you have a gap.

Designing a Career Path

Career paths are natural progressions for individuals within a specific job function. As an employee gains experience and expertise they can move to the next level where they have expanded responsibilities. For instance, you might have an entry-level position of Web Designer. The next step might be Webmaster, then Web Designer & Developer, and so on up to Software Architect or Director of Software Initiatives.

It is important to clearly show the difference between levels so that employees know what they must do to get to move up in the organization. Look at the sample in Figure 8-1 for the path from Data Entry Clerk to Office Manager. The competencies listed are not exhaustive, but should give you an idea of how an individual advances from one level to the next by building competencies, experience and education.

Figure 8-1 Career Path Samples

Job Title	Education	Experience	Competencies
Data Entry Clerk	High School Diploma	1-3 years general work experience	• Accuracy • Speed • Teamwork • Complete assigned task with direction • Basic computer skills
Administrative Assistant	Associate Degree	3+ years office experience	• Complete assigned tasks with minimal direction • Advanced computer skills to include spreadsheets, databases, word processing

Administrative Lead	4-year College Degree	5+ years office experience	• Project management • Attention to detail • Ability to motivate others • Time management
Office Manager	4-year College Degree	5+ years office experience, proven leadership experience	• Ability to manage the work of others • Ability to prioritize work • Confidence • Initiative

It is important to know the career goals and interests of your employees. Some people are satisfied with their current role and have no interest in advancement. If that is the case, look for ways to use their expertise in their current role to help others in the organization. It is a good idea to ask individuals during their annual performance discussion what their latest goals are. A lot can happen in a year, and they may have changed their minds or have new ideas. If their goals are unrealistic it is important to share what you envision for them early on so that they can adjust their plan.

For instance, you may have someone hired in an office position that has expressed an interest in sales. If you see that they have the potential to do well in sales, you might consider ways to give them experience, such as joining a current salesperson on presentations, working on a cross-functional team to get more exposure to sales, or providing them with resources to help explore sales as a career path. Go back through the required competencies for the position and compare the individual's strengths to determine if they have the potential to succeed in a career shift.

On the other hand, if they express an interest in sales and you do not see a good fit, you should provide alternatives and explore what it is that interests them about sales and how they may incorporate some sales-like tasks within their current career path. If they are attracted to the compensation opportunities in sales but do not have the personality to succeed in a sales position within your organization, talk with them about advancement opportunities that align better with their strengths.

There are two parts to having a good career path for your organization: First, plan ahead to identify levels within each functional area (Sales, Administration, Customer Service, Information Technology, etc.) and what the unique experience and competency requirements are for each level. Second: align your hiring practices with your career paths. Start by putting the right person in the right job and you will have a much easier time managing progression of individuals from one level to the next.

As your organization starts to grow and find it necessary to add staff, begin thinking about additional skills you need someone to have. Is it better to promote the person that's been with you for a while and bring in someone at a lower position to learn from them? Or does the person that has been with you from the beginning lack the technical expertise you need to advance your organization? These are questions you have to consider as you grow and expand your business.

Succession Planning

The Society for Human Resource Management (SHRM) defines succession planning as

> The process of identifying high-potential employees, evaluating and honing their skills and abilities, and preparing them for advancement into positions which are key to the success of business operations and objectives. (2008, Society for Human Resource Management)

Succession planning is a leadership strategy that creates a plan for replacing key individuals as they advance to new positions or leave your organization altogether. Companies who do succession planning well use career pathing to continuously feed the talent pipeline so that people are intentionally hired to supply the succession funnel. If you have someone you are grooming for management, who is ready to step into their role once they are promoted? This is especially important for top-level leadership positions. If you lose your VP of Sales to competition or tragedy, who can step in immediately to keep the ball rolling?

There are various templates and tools available to help leaders create a succession plan. A popular and flexible tool is the Nine Box grid (Illustration 8-2). You don't have to have a large team to benefit from this simple approach. The grid will help you get a pretty good picture of who is ready for promotion and who needs to be coached or developed, or possibly separated from your organization.

First, set your criteria. Decide what is important to you. Think about what the most successful individual in a given role does. Take, for instance, accounting. Your star performer, whether it be a VP of finance, CFO, or lead accountant, is probably extremely knowledgeable about corporate finance, understands all of the legal requirements and best accounting practices. But a star finance person will proactively look for ways to manage expenses, not just keep the books. They negotiate contracts for the best pricing and have the company's best interest in mind. They may even have ideas related to revenue generation and product development because they are fully engaged in your business. It's more than just a job to them – they are part of the company.

On the other hand, your low potential, low performance finance person is closer to a bookkeeper, but struggles to meet deadlines, needs constant supervision, and regularly makes mistakes. If you judge that they have some potential, even though their current performance is low, you will need to develop a plan to help them not only gain the required skills, but develop the accountability, engagement and proactive nature of your star performer. You may be able to move them up a few boxes, possibly to a core employee level, but they may never be the star that you want to be in charge of your company's books.

Figure 8-2 Nine Box Grid

	Low	Medium	High	
High	7 Professional Subject Expert	8 Agile High-Performer	9 Star	High
Performance	4 Solid Performer	5 Core Employee	6 Rising Star	Medium
	1 Termination Risk	2 Inconsistent Performer	3 Potential Gem	Low

Potential/Promotability ⟶

Rule of Thumb:
It is important show a clear career path, or various options that might be open to employee's so that they know what must be done to get ahead in the organization.

If you have a staff of high performing, high potential employees, but only one top spot, you will need to consider how to keep everyone engaged.

Can you expand or rotate responsibilities? Is there a way to build specializations to help hone skills even further? It is a good thing to have high performing, promotable employees, but if you have no promotional opportunities for them they may compete with another or look outside of your company for the challenge they need. If you want to keep them, you will have to provide a structure, reward system, and culture that allows them to use their strengths and not waste their potential.

Use scorecards and performance data to help you put people in the right box. Look at performance over time – at least 6 months – to get a good understanding of the ups and downs of the individual's average productivity. Do you see patterns of improved performance? You will want to watch to see if the trend continues and provide encouragement when you see an upswing in performance. Talk with the employee about what they are doing differently that has led to performance improvement. The same principle applies to those experiencing lagging performance – what has changed? Do they swing from exceeding goals to underperforming? An inconsistency in performance needs to be analyzed to see if the problem is with the employee or the process.

Succession planning should not be a secret activity. Those you are considering for advancement should be aware of your interest in promoting them, even if it is in the distant future. It not only assures them that you have noticed their performance and potential, but gives them hope and a desire to commit themselves to the organization. You may even find that they are not interested in advancing, or had ideas to move into another area of the company. Being transparent with your staff promotes trust in your organization. When people know where they stand, they can focus on work rather than office politics.

The annual performance appraisal meeting is an excellent time to have a discussion about the employee's career path and promotion potential. Get the employee's buy-in and ask for them to develop a plan to gain additional skills and abilities. Perhaps the only thing holding them back from a promotion is lack of formal education. Talk about ways you could modify their schedule so that they can take classes or attend seminars.

Succession planning, or succession development as some call it, is really a process of managing talent. Having a defined process, including clear measurements of performance, what you need at each level of a job category, and how you plan to work with employees to develop them to the next level, will ensure talent is recognized and promoted in a way that makes sense. When employees know what it takes to advance, and you commit to using those guidelines and not promote based on personality or friendship, then they can focus on doing their best for your organization.

Chapter 9
Positive Discipline

Traditional discipline processes put the burden on managers to come up with the solution to an employee's poor performance. Discipline Without Punishment, or what I like to call "Positive Discipline," places the burden for performance on the employee, asking them to commit to a plan for success that they design to meet the needs of the business. The process was introduced by Dick Grote in the 1970s, and has been applied in companies large and small around the world.

Positive Discipline makes performance improvement a much more constructive process. Most of us are used to the traditional progressive discipline process of verbal warning, written warning, final warning and termination. We would call this "discipline WITH punishment!" The message this approach sends to employees is "you are on your way out." It puts them on the defensive and requires the supervisor to be the heavy. Both sides feel a great deal of stress and pain, which does little to motivate the employee to improve performance (except out of fear of job loss) or the manager to cooperate to help the employee succeed.

Figure 9-1 Traditional Discipline Process

Informal Transactions

Coaching/Counseling

Formal Disciplinary Process

- Step 1: Oral Warning
- Step 2: Written Warning
- Step 3: Suspension Without Pay/Final Warning/Probation
- Step 4: Termination

Figure 9-2 Positive Discipline (Without Punishment)

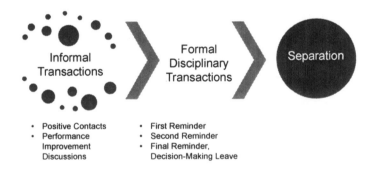

Informal Transactions

Formal Disciplinary Transactions

Separation

- Positive Contacts
- Performance Improvement Discussions

- First Reminder
- Second Reminder
- Final Reminder, Decision-Making Leave

Positive Discipline is a process that promotes cooperation between the employee who is not meeting expectations and the supervisor who really needs a high-performing staff. Notice in illustration 9-2 the difference in language between the traditional approach and Positive Discipline. Instead of "warnings" you have "reminders" and "termination" becomes "separation." Before you think Positive Discipline is a soft approach, let's look at the process more closely to see how the accountability is put on the underperforming employee.

The starting place for discipline should not be when the employee falls short. Whether a policy violation, missed sales goal, or some other performance deficiency, in Positive Discipline performance dialogue begins with coaching. When you have regular performance coaching meetings with your staff, issues are addressed immediately before they become negative patterns or larger problems. Recognizing positive trends and discussing shortfalls as they occur means you may never have to go to a formal process at all.

If, however, a negative trend persists, you have a reminder discussion with the employee. Because you have already communicated clearly what the expectations are, you are simply reminding them of those expectations and asking them to comply. Coaching has not motivated them to change their behavior, so you are reminding them of the guidelines and getting their commitment to do what they promised to do.

Provide facts and visual illustrations whenever possible. For instance, if they have a sales goal of five thousand dollars per week, write that goal at the top of a sheet of paper. Then write down what their actual performance has been for the last few weeks, leaving plenty of "white space" to make it obvious that there is a gap between the two numbers. Highlight the gap and ask them what they will do to close it. Ask them what they think is getting in the way of achieving the goal. Get them to identify what they could do differently to improve their sales performance. It is important not to answer for them. Stay silent while they think, either to themselves or aloud, about what they need to do. This is one of the main differences between the traditional discipline process and Grote's Discipline Without Punishment. In the traditional progressive model the supervisor fills out a form and gives direction to the employee about the causes and solutions to the performance gap.

Rule of Thumb –
When employees have to develop their own improvement plan, they are much more likely to accomplish it. They will have ownership and you can hold them accountable for achieving what they said they would.

When an employee has to develop their own improvement plan, they are much more likely to accomplish it. They will have ownership and you can hold them accountable for achieving what they said they would. It takes the pressure off the supervisor and puts it where it belongs, with the underperforming employee. Your job, then, is one of fine-tuning the plan and providing feedback on their progress. In fine-tuning, use questions to help them make the plan realistic and manageable. Get them to think about measurable goals, not general phrases like, "get better" "work harder" or "spend more time." What do they mean by that? What, specifically, will they do? And if they present goals that don't seem realistic, based on their current performance, help them to create a multi-step plan that you can work with them on.

Employees want to succeed. They want to meet goals. Sometimes personal circumstances and distractions get them off track. Most will step up and make the necessary corrections when you take a positive approach with them. Sometimes, though, they just can't seem to get back on track. Their skills and abilities may have peaked, which could be an indication of a poor hiring decision. Or they may have decided the position is not a good fit for them, but are reluctant to quit until they have another position. Essentially, they are riding your payroll while they look elsewhere. Whatever the case, when a person does not make the necessary improvements after a second reminder discussion, it's time for them to make a decision.

Discipline Without Punishment uses a decision-making leave to allow the person a day or two to think about what they want to do. While the traditional progressive discipline model uses suspension without pay, the decision-making leave is paid time off with a specific outcome. The task of the employee during the leave is to weigh their options and commitment and come back at the end of the leave to let the supervisor know if they are committed to their job. If they are, great! You can develop a plan with them and hold them accountable going forward. They could decide that they really are not committed and it's time to separate from the company.

The scenario below illustrates how Positive Discipline should work.

Karl has been on the job for six months and is struggling to meet some of the requirements of his job as inventory clerk consistently and within the quality standards.

His supervisor, Mindy, has provided formal and informal feedback through positive contacts and performance improvement discussions. Although Karl has improved in some areas, Mindy is still concerned about his understanding of what to do with damages and overages.

The time has come to begin formal disciplinary transactions, which means Mindy will remind Karl of the importance of handling damages and overages and the financial consequences the company has if not done properly. Mindy lets Karl know where his performance stands compared to the expectations and asks him how he plans to close the gap.

At this point the ball is in Karl's court. He is

being asked to come up with a solution, not handed a solution by Mindy. Karl believes that a brief job-aid that visually reminds him about the processes will fix the problem. Mindy supports this solution and pairs Karl up with another employee who handles damages and overages properly to create the job aid. Before the meeting is over, Mindy asks Karl for his commitment and sets a follow-up meeting for the next week.

If Karl either did not follow through on the job aid, or it did not help him to do the job correctly, Mindy would talk to him during their follow-up meeting about ways to tweak the solution. This would happen 1-2 times, and in most cases significant improvement is made.

But sometimes an employee will respond negatively no matter how much help is offered or how much input they have in the solution. In these cases the supervisor would jump to the decision-making leave step, giving the employee 24 hours to decide whether or not they are committed to keeping their job.

The good news is that Karl's solution worked and he is quickly becoming a highly productive and efficient worker. The Positive Discipline process made it possible for Karl to receive the guidance he needed while putting the accountability on him to close his performance gap. He did not have to respond defensively because Mindy had regularly let him know what he was doing well and partnered with him to solve the problem with handling damages and overages correctly.

Chapter 10
Closing Performance Gaps

Performance barriers pop up for a variety of reasons. We often respond to poor performance with either strong discipline or more training. As we discussed in the previous chapter, there is a right way to do discipline and coaching that gets people back on track. But there are times when you have to look beyond the individual and see what is in the "system" that could be contributing to the less-than-desirable results.

In their book Analyzing Performance Problems: Or, You Really Oughta Wanna – How to Figure out Why People Aren't Doing What They Should Be, and What to do About It , Robert Mager and Peter Pipe introduce a process of sorting through the performance information that is available to get to a solution that addresses the issues.

The best place to start is with a summary of the performance gap. This is very similar to the process used in Positive Discipline. You need to know what performance is supposed to look like, then compare the individual's performance against that standard. That difference between what is and what ought to be is your discrepancy, or performance gap. When production numbers, sales goals, or other measurements are used, this can be fairly simple to identify: Sales goal = $2500/week. Actual = $1800/week. You have a gap of $700. Of course, you want to look at this over a period of time, not just the first time it happens. Once a pattern of performance has been identified, then you can move to the next question.

It may seem like a stupid question, but it is surprising how much we hold people accountable for that does not really matter! So we ask the question, "is it important?" Does whether they do such-and-such really matter? Does it impact the bottom line, improve customer service, or is it a carry-over from "the way we've always done things" that no longer has a purpose? If so, stop the madness! Eliminate it from the expectations and move on.

Sometimes performance is important, but maybe not in the way it is being measured. Or you may find out that a change is necessary to do work more efficiently, such as automating a routine task that has always been done manually.

If you have found out that the performance gap really is important, then it is time to move to the next item in the flow diagram: Is there a skill deficiency? This is the point where you want to find out if this is a "will" or "skill" issue. If it's a skill issue, we want to dig into when & how they were trained and how frequently they used the skill. But we may determine that it's more of a "will" issue. We know they can do the job, but for some reason they are pulling back on their performance, missing deadlines, not meeting quality standards, and so on.

Let's assume that it's a skill issue. The next thing to find out is if they ever did the task before. If the answer is no, then you want to set up some training for them. If they did do it at one time, how often is the task done? If this is a once-a-quarter or once-a-year process, then you may need to arrange for a refresher shortly before it is scheduled again, and provide coaching. Another good option is to create some written instructions, preferably an easy step-by-step guide or checklist.

If it is something they do often but they are under-performing, you want to evaluate the procedures to see if there is an easier way. Is this the first person who has struggled with the task or do you regularly find yourself coaching employees on it? Always be on the lookout for ways to simplify processes. And listen to the employees who do the job – what are their frustrations? What ideas do they have to make it easier, more efficient, or replace the process altogether? If you do end up changing the process, make sure everyone who does the job gets trained on the new procedures.

You may get to the point where you have to ask whether the person has potential. It is difficult to admit when we make bad hiring decisions, but for the sake of your business and the long-term satisfaction of the employee, it could be the best solution is to move the person to a job that is a better fit or separate from them if you have no positions that fit their strengths and abilities.

If you have determined that skill and ability are not the problem, then you are dealing with a will issue. So the next step in the performance analysis is to figure out what attitudes, processes, or policies might be contributing to the employee's lack of desire to fully perform the job.

Mager and Pipe identify four possible issues:

1. Is performance punishing?
2. Is non-performance rewarding?
3. Does performance matter?
4. Are their obstacles to performance?

Asking the question, "is performance punishing?" brings to light managerial practices or organizational culture issues that may lead to unintended outcomes. In some workplaces, for example, it is punishing to meet or exceed quota because it makes everyone else look bad. When a shining new star begins to out-perform co-workers, they may be subject to hostility, harassment, or even sabotage. When leaders discover these punishing practices, they need to carefully adjust things within the system to remove the punishment and create greater buy-in from the team.

Rule of Thumb:
Always be on the lookout for ways to simplify processes. And listen to the employees who do the job.

Another example of punishing performance is when someone goes above and beyond to win a client, meet a deadline, or clean up a mess and they receive no recognition for their extra efforts. If this practice is widespread and ongoing, employees quickly become disengaged and underperforming because it isn't worth it to them.

The opposite side of the coin is when non-performance is rewarding. In other words, it may actually pay to under-perform. For example, if a standard is set too low, or there are no clear-cut goals, employees may give minimal effort and experience no negative consequences. Or if focus is put on a single aspect of the job but other aspects go un-measured, inefficiency and underperformance abound. A sales contest that rewards quantity over quality of service may see aggressive salespeople winning coveted awards but client satisfaction and co-worker morale may suffer.

To turn things around, managers need to put positive consequences in place that rewards desired performance. A well-worn saying is "you get what you measure." This is certainly true for employee performance, and employees are looking to managers to tell them, either directly or indirectly, what is important.

Next we want to look at the question, "does performance matter?" This is tied to our first question at the top of the flow chart, "is it important?" As we drill down to discover why a gap exists, we have to ask questions about what we are measuring. Are there metrics left over from an old process that need to be removed, or steps that are becoming obsolete due to new technology or ways of getting the job done? One of the benefits of doing a systematic and system-wide performance analysis is that it allows for a broader look at processes, procedures and policies that may need to be updated.

If performance matters and you have identified specific tasks and performance goals (KPIs), make sure they are clear to employees and let them know the consequences for not performing to standards. Remember, consequences are both negative and positive. How can you make it unpleasant to miss standards and rewarding to meet/exceed them?

Finally, we want to ask the question, "are there obstacles to performance?" Performance obstacles come from three primary sources:

Technical: It is difficult to keep up with technology advancements when new version of both software and hardware are released every couple of years. At some point technology could be holding employees back from meeting performance expectations. If your system can only process 100 units per hour and your goal is 125, no one will be able to make that goal. Employees and managers alike will become frustrated. On the other end of the spectrum, always look for ways to automate processes so that people can be freed up to use their time and talents for more useful activities.

Human: Human obstacles often come in the form of mediocre supervisors. We have a tendency to promote people who have performed well in production to supervision, and realize quickly that they do not have the skills to lead others. Another human obstacle is when supervisors are overloaded with responsibilities and they cannot effectively manage their employees.

Policy/Procedure: Organizations often hinder performance by putting too many rules in place that don't add value to the process. Multiple approvals, double-checking, and meaningless reports get in the way and negatively impact morale. Remove layers and streamline processes to keep things moving forward. Empower workers and look for ways to tear down obstacles that stand in the way.

The value of following the performance analysis process is in taking a serious look at what is impacting your employees' ability to do their jobs well. Your job as a manager is to clear the way, equip, and encourage peak performance. The key elements of performance success are clearly stated expectations, proper training and onboarding (initial training/orientation), accountability, recognition, and continuous evaluation and improvement.

Once you develop a solution to a performance problem it is important to implement well, and then evaluate to see if the solution did what it was supposed to. Additional tweaking may be required, so avoid the temptation to put something in place and assume the problem is fixed.

If you build a culture that implements this performance analysis on a regular basis, employees will become a part of the evaluation process and will proactively look for ways to close performance gaps. Of course, part of the culture-building requires managers to remain open to ideas and feedback. If you want fully engaged employees, include them in designing their jobs, making improvements, and rewarding their input.

Chapter 11
When and How to Terminate an Employee

Bad hiring decisions are not the end of the world. There is often a lot of drama that comes as a consequence of putting the wrong person in a job, but when handled well both parties can come away scar-free!

Terminating with TACT

I try to avoid acronyms because there are so many, and often they seem forced, but I think TACT is a worthy acronym to use when terminating an employee. It is a reminder to be considerate, kind, and professional no matter what the circumstances.

Before you get to the point of terminating with TACT, you first have to decide that it is time to sever ties with the employee. Call it what you will: terminate, separate, fire, sever, but it all comes down to a realization that the employment relationship cannot continue. Whether for will or skill, performance or attitude, when an employee shows no signs of improvement, the longer you keep them employed the more damage you will likely do to your organization through lost productivity and lower morale.

For most terminations, the Positive Discipline process works well because it puts the responsibility on the employee to improve or, basically, terminate themselves. It also gives you a chance to consider moving them to another role that might be suited better fit for them.

But sometimes a single incident may warrant immediate termination, usually because of willful negligence (they just didn't care enough to do the right thing) or illegal activity. Ethical misconduct does not typically warrant a second chance, nor does mistreatment of clients, co-workers or supervisors.

Whatever leads up to it, terminating an employee ranks as one of the most unpleasant tasks for any manager. To make a difficult responsibility as positive and painless as possible, follow the four principles of TACT.

Tact is defined as the "**ability to avoid giving offense:** skill in situations in which other people's feelings have to be considered." (Bing). Tact is synonymous with diplomacy, sensitivity, thoughtfulness, and discernment. Even though you may feel the person being fired does not deserve your respect or sensitivity because of their own poor behavior and performance, it is essential for any manager of people to learn to deliver the harshest of news with tact and professionalism.

So let's discover the principles of tact that will make the termination experience as professional as possible:

T – Transparency. It is important to be honest and open with the employee. The decision to terminate should not be a surprise to the employee. If you have followed the Discipline Without Punishment process and regularly updated the employee on how they are performing, they are aware if their job is in jeopardy.

A – Appreciation. Our identity is often closely tied to our job. Losing a job takes a huge emotional toll, affecting self-esteem and our ability to see the situation in perspective. Make an effort to appreciate the talents and contributions the employee has made. Express your gratitude for any effort that they took to improve their performance.

C – Coaching. Coaching may seem like an odd element of terminating someone, but it is a valuable mindset for creating a positive experience for both you and the employee being fired. As a leader, you have a natural position as coach and counselor. While you want to resist the urge to lecture or beat a dead horse, you do want to give wise counsel about where the employee might begin their job search. Tell them where you see them excelling and give 2-3 bits of advice that are non-judgmental and positive.

T – Thoughtfulness. The best way to apply thoughtfulness in a termination meeting is to put yourself in the other person's shoes. How would you want to be treated if you had either been unable to perform according to the requirements of the job, or had made a mistake that warranted your being fired?

The Golden Rule is still a relevant guide for us today – to treat others the way we want to be treated. And how does anyone want to be treated? With respect, kindness, and understanding. We're all human and make mistakes. Be gracious no matter what led to a decision to fire someone.

The Termination Meeting

Experts can't agree on the best time to terminate someone. Many will say Monday morning, so the person has the week to go out and begin their job search right away. Others will say that it should be Friday afternoon, so that they have the weekend to process before the new week begins. This option also reduces the likelihood that the person may come back to the office in a fit of rage.

If you're the person being fired, there is probably no good time! Certainly a termination for any cause that includes violence, safety or security should be done rather quickly. But in most cases it is best not to rush to the termination meeting without preparing beforehand.

Rule of Thumb:
State the facts so that the employee knows exactly why you are severing employment. Termination should not be a surprise to them.

To be ready for the meeting, you should:

- Make sure you have covered all of the legal bases before terminating. What are the likely repercussions from the person being fired, their co-workers, and others in the company?
- Clearly identify what guidelines have been violated, the cause for termination. Make sure all documentation is gathered about performance and behavior.
- It is best to have two company representatives present in the meeting, typically the person's supervisor and a senior manager or human resources manager. It provides a witness for any future accusations and a "safety in numbers" atmosphere in case the person is tempted to react violently to the news. However, only one person should do the majority of the talking, so that the person does not feel ganged up on.
- Know what benefits, pay, and other entitlements are available for the employee. If possible, have their final paycheck available to hand them, along with any documentation for COBRA insurance or other types of benefits continuation. Your goal is to try to preempt the need for the employee to continue communication with the company.
- Let the employee know if and when they are eligible for re-hire. Do you have a policy

that clearly outlines the types of behavior that render a person ineligible for future employment with your company? Is your policy consistently applied in all cases? If not, you may be opening yourself up to Equal Employment Opportunity Commission (EEOC) risk.

The important thing with terminations is to be consistent, clear, and tactful. State the facts so that the employee knows why you are severing employment. This is not the time to beat around the bush. Reduce tension and animosity by remaining calm and professional throughout the termination meeting. Resist the urge to counsel and lecture. Maintain respect for the individual even while you inform them that they are no longer employed. Terminating with TACT makes the best of a trying situation.

Chapter 12
Continuous Improvement

Following the guidelines for performance management found in this book will chart a course for success for your organization, for you as a manager, and for your employees as individual contributors. Managing employee performance is no easy thing, and you may feel overwhelmed by the processes and data required to make performance management effective and efficient. It is important to see performance management as a process, and one that is constantly changing.

Start with one or two areas and, once you feel they are in good shape, focus on another area. You will have to decide for yourself which of the ten functions of performance management will give you the best return on your investment of time, money, and attention. I suggest completing a brief assessment, using a simple scale to determine how you are doing in each function. Figure 12-2 provides an example of a simple assessment that might help you determine where to start.

You will likely want to start with the areas that you rated Mostly Ineffective or Highly Ineffective, since any positive improvements in those areas are likely to have immediately positive impact on your work group. You could also start with the items in the Moderately Effective column, since you will have a sense of immediate satisfaction in taking them to a Mostly Effective or Highly Effective rating with only moderate effort. Once you have the boost in confidence, you can turn toward the functions marked lowest.

The good news is, any attention you give to improving your performance management efforts is likely to have a positive effect on your organization. Employees will notice the extra effort and will appreciate the constructive changes you are making. Sure, you may have some cynical employees who will wait to see if the focus will last. That is why it is important to stick with it over time.

Figure 12-1 Performance Management Assessment

Performance Management Function	Highly Effective	Mostly Effective	Moderately Effective	Mostly Ineffective	Highly Ineffective
Defining Staffing Needs					
Right Person, Right Job					
Knowing What to Measure – KPIs					
Recognizing and Rewarding Contributions					
Coaching & Accountability					
Formal Performance Appraisals					
Career Paths & Succession Plans					
Positive Discipline					
Closing Performance Gaps					
When & How to Terminate					

Engaging Employees

One of the best ways to ensure employees are on board with your performance management efforts is to involve them in the process. Share some of your ideas with them and get feedback. Be careful not to promise anything, and frame the discussion with a "disclaimer" that states you are looking for ways to positively manage performance and want their feedback and input. The key to this type of involvement is being clear on parameters, expectations, and how you will evaluate their suggestions.

Employees may have some great ideas that you think make a lot of sense and can quickly incorporate into your performance management process. Other ideas may be less-than-inspired, but how you respond will make a world of difference. If there is a way to use even a piece of their suggestion, you will build a great deal of trust and goodwill. If it is not possible, you will need to explain why you cannot use their idea at this time, being specific and encouraging. Just because one idea could not be used, you want them to continue bringing suggestions. Use it as a teaching/coaching opportunity.

Build Your Understanding

Continuous improvement requires that you make a commitment to building your understanding of performance management. Whether that means perusing this book again in a few months, attending a conference, or talking with other managers about what they have found most successful when it comes to managing employee performance, keep learning new things that will make you a more effective manager.

Continuous improvement is also an excellent way to model the way for your employees. By showing them that you are always learning, continuously trying new ways to improve yourself and the organization, you will create an organizational culture that looks at continuous improvement as "the way we do things around here."

Conclusion

Performance management is important. How you set the tone for employees has a direct impact on your organization's success. Creating a plan for adding staff, ensuring you hire the right people for the right job, measuring the key performance indicators, and holding employees accountable for meeting expectations leads to accomplishment of your organizational goals. Without an effective performance management process you risk falling short of your objectives.

It may seem like a lot of work, and you may find it worth the expense to hire a consultant to help you get a performance management plan set up. You may find that your next hire should be a human resources professional, someone who could work directly with you and your team to move you in the right direction with people management. If you are not ready for either of these steps, look for ways to incorporate performance management into your responsibilities.

One of the most eye-opening activities is that of identifying metrics for jobs. Even with the simplest job description, you can begin to make a list of what measurements make sense for that role. And once you begin to track how people are doing against the goals, you will discover that you have some gaps. It may be that the goals are too high and no one can achieve them, at least not with the system currently in place. You may also see that one person consistently outperforms everyone else. Find out what that person is doing differently and get the rest of the team following suit, Highly motivated, smart people always find a way to succeed. Leverage that ability by teaching others to do things the same way.

I hope you have found this book useful, and that you will return to it from time-to-time as you continuously evaluate and work to improve your ability to manage your staff. I encourage you to get a copy of the books I referenced, especially Discipline Without Punishment and Analyzing Performance Problems. Keep your eyes and ears open for ways to enhance your performance management efforts. You will see a valuable return on your investment!

Appendix A
Competencies

Note: As you consider which of the following competencies are required for a particular position in your organization, think about how you define the item. For instance, "negotiating" may mean something very specific to you, but something very different to your partner. Come to agreement on how you define each competency. You may also identify competencies not listed here. This list is just to get you started. A Google search of competencies will likely lead to some definitions that already exist. You may also want to check out the Lominger (Korn/Ferry) book, FYI: For Your Improvement, that provides greater detail on competencies and how to use them.

Rule of Thumb

□ Accountability	□ Empowering Others	□ Managing Risk
□ Analytical Thinking	□ Entrepreneurship	□ Negotiating
□ Building Trust	□ Establishing Focus	□ Organizational Communications
□ Change Management	□ Exercising Self-Control /Being Resilient	□ Partnering/ Networking
□ Coaching	□ Facilitation	□ Political Skill
□ Communicating in Writing	□ Fiscal Management	□ Project Management
□ Communicating Orally	□ Flexibility	□ Providing Direction
□ Conflict Management	□ Getting Results	□ Providing Motivational Support
□ Continual Learning	□ Influencing Others	□ Solving Problems
□ Continual Improvement	□ Initiative	□ Systems Thinking
□ Customer Focus	□ Innovation	□ Technical Credibility
□ Decision Making	□ Interpersonal Skills	□ Technology Use/ Management
□ Delegation	□ Listening	□ Thinking Strategically
□ Developing Others	□ Maintaining Personal Credibility/ Meeting Ethical Standards	□ Valuing and Leveraging Diversity
□ Emotional Intelligence	□ Managing Performance	□ Visioning

Bibliography

Buckingham, M. (2011). StandOut: The Groundbreaking New Strengths Assessment from the Leader of the Strengths Revolution. Nashville: THOMAS NELSON.

Grote, R. (2006). Discipline Without Punishment: The Proven Strategy That Turns Problem Employees Into Superior Performers. New York: AMACOM; 2nd edition.

Lombardo, M. M. (2009). *FYI: For Your Improvement - For Learners, Managers, Mentors, and Feedback Givers* . Minneapolis: LOMINGER INTERNATIONAL; 5th edition.

Mager, R. & Pipe, P. (1997). Analyzing Performance Problems: Or, You Really Oughta Wanna - How to Figure Out Why People Aren't Doing What They Should Be, and What to do About It. Atlanta: CENTER FOR EFFECTIVE PERFORMANCE; 3rd edition.

Author's Biography

 Todd Conkright's career has always centered on helping individuals and organizations identify and close the gap between what is and what ought to be. As a human capital strategist, human performance analyst, instructional designer and learning facilitator he has helped organizations maximize their greatest asset: their people.

Before starting his consulting practice, Cornerstone Global Training & Performance Solutions, Todd was an internal consultant for companies of 200 to 25,000 employees, initiating and implementing creative solutions to challenging performance issues. An intuitive problem solver, Todd has been instrumental in reducing turnover, improving talent sourcing, increasing knowledge retention and optimizing the customer experience.

Todd earned a bachelor's degree in HR Management from Grace University and a master's in Organizational Development Consulting from

Regent University. He is Past-President of the Omaha Organization Development Network board and an adjunct instructor of human resource management.

Todd can be reached at todd@cornerstoneglobaltps.com or 402-650-4921.

You can also follow him on Twitter: @GapMinding or LinkedIn: www.linkedin.com/in/toddconkright/

Rule of Thumb
Small Business Book Series

Please enjoy these other titles from the Rule of Thumb for Business book series!

A Small Business Guide to Sales Strategy
Author: Jill Slupe

This book shares practical methods that can be used to accelerate sales in business. It leads new and existing business owners through the sales process and lays the groundwork for a sound sales strategy that serves as a foundation for successful business. Strategic and tactical exercises push the reader to create actual business strategies that drive revenue.   Book ISBN: 978-1-60808-060-1

A Small Business Guide to Customer Service and Relationships
Author: Lisa Tschauner

This book is designed as a tool for the small business owner. Through identifying customers, their needs and wants, successful communication strategies, methods for follow-up and best practices, anyone who is involved in a business environment can build outstanding and valuable relationships with customers and clients. Readers will be guided through the developing dynamic and unique strategies that are sure to grow their business. Book ISBN: 978-1-60808-066-3

A Small Business Guide to Basics
Authors: Marian Shalander Kaiser and Michael Mitilier

As the initial book in the series, this guide will assist you in gaining a basic understanding of what it takes to operate a small business. It discusses the legal requirements, financial resources, record-keeping requirements, ways to market the business, communication skills, human resource laws, as well as issues that may arise on a day-to-day basis. Book ISBN: 978-1-60808-024-3

A Small Business Guide to Marketing
Author: David Catalan

This is an introductory guide for the first-time entrepreneur starting a new small business, as well as for an existing business owner who wants to grow and needs marketing advice. The author describes the essential, need-to-know concepts which combine to drive strategic directions toward success. Real world and commonly understood examples and experiences help the reader identify the strengths which underscore a healthy marketing business plan. Book ISBN: 978-1-60808-047-2

A Small Business Guide to Growth
Author: Linda Swalling Fettig

Business growth is an exciting and often very hectic time in the life cycle of a business. This easy to read book helps entrepreneurs understand business growth and the impact it has. Readers will learn how to work "on" their business even as they are busy working "in" their business. Book ISBN: 978-1-60808-062-5

A Small Business Guide to Marketing Yourself for Success
Author: Rita Rocker

In today's competitive business environment, good manners, proper speech patterns, a dynamic appearance, professional communication and networking skills can make the difference between getting ahead and being left behind. Readers will learn how to build a successful, personal brand, NOW! Book ISBN: 978-1-60808-048-9

A Small Business Guide to Communication Basics for Owners and Managers
Author: Marian Shalander Kaiser

This book provides basic information to help you improve both written and oral communication skills. It shows you how to be kind to your readers by making what you've written easy to understand. Book ISBN: 978-1-60808-046-5

A Small Business Guide to Sustainability
Author: Dr. Beverly Ann Browning

This title closes the "how-to stay in business" information gap for micro and small businesses that are struggling to last beyond today's reactive approaches. It is for readers who have a vision of their business lasting forever. This guide show the action steps for diversifying revenues, lasting in the social media market, branding smarter, finding new revenue streams, and planning for business succession. Book ISBN: 978-1608080533

A Small Business Guide to Peak Performance Through People
Author: Todd Conkright

This brief guide provides practical insights that any manager of people will find useful. It introduces a simple process to ensure your organization achieves peak performance by selecting, managing and developing individuals who are aligned with your organization's goals. Book ISBN: 978-1608080779

The Rule of Thumb for Business book series is a collective of expert advice and guidance from industry professionals. These authors include the some of the best minds in today's business world. The books are easy to read and full of applicable information that will benefit any entrepreneur, manager or business leader.

Please visit the Rule of Thumb for Business website at www.ruleofthumbbiz.com to learn more information about this organization, contact us or to order additional books. The Rule of Thumb authors are also available for speaking engagements, conference workshops or for educational training purposes. Details and contact information for each author can be found on the website.

CPSIA information can be obtained at www.ICGtesting.com
Printed in the USA
BVOW05s1453150514

353488BV00002B/3/P

9 781608 080779